Dancing Through Fields of Color

by
Elizabeth Brown

illustrations by
Aimée Sicuro

The Story of Helen Frankenthaler

ABRAMS BOOKS FOR YOUNG READERS • NEW YORK

At a time when girls were taught to sit still, learn their manners, and color inside the lines, Helen Frankenthaler colored her reds, blues, and yellows any which way she chose.

Helen never wanted to follow the rules.

When her mother called her to the dinner table,
Helen continued painting watercolors of the sunset
shining through the apartment window.

Instead of going to bed, Helen filled the sink with water. She dribbled in drops of ruby red nail polish and watched the color flow. When she let the water out, she loved to watch the color swirl into shapes.

During summer vacations, Helen let the waves *whoosh* and *whirl* around her, sailing her body through the tides. When her father called her ashore, she wanted to keep . . .

circling

twisting

floating

. . . forever wrapped in the blue-green colors of the sea.

While her older sisters were in school, Helen spent her days with her mother who nurtured her dreams. Helen read and wrote stories, made collages, and created designs with glass beads—circles, hearts, and stars in brilliant colors. She painted pictures and cards for birthdays and anniversaries, filled with all the colors of happiness: purple, yellow, and pink.

Helen's father worked long days as a judge.
She couldn't wait for him to come home
each day. He took her wherever
she wanted to go.

Most of all, Helen loved taking walks with her family in Central Park. She ran under the welcoming sky . . .

waltzing

twirling

leaping

. . . across the lush green fields, and played hide-and-seek among the flowering trees. When it was time to go, Helen took the colored chalk she had stuffed in her coat pockets and drew a line from the front of the Metropolitan Museum of Art through the park,

across the street,

and through the crowds,

around the corner,

all the way home.

The colorful line connected the two things she loved most.
Helen's parents always encouraged her to
blossom,
express herself,
paint free.

In art class at school, Helen wanted
to do things her way, but she had to
follow the rules in order to pass.

Don't sketch that way! Draw like this!
Paint what you see!

Helen pleased her teachers
when she sketched figures,
drew chairs, and painted
flowers and pears like all
the other students.

But she wished for something different.

Helen found comfort in painting seascapes. The blues and greens reminded her of summer days with her family at the beach. She made pictures of her trips to the country, with bursts of orange-gold paints that warmed her face like the sun.

Soon Helen's happiness disappeared entirely. When she was eleven, her father died. Helen missed him so much that her sadness caused pounding headaches. She struggled in school. Helen tried painting, but nothing came out.

Her canvases remained blank,
her world of colors and light . . .
dark.

But colors lived in her mind, floating and shifting like the shapes she made in childhood. Staring at every color in her paint box, memories came back to her:

periwinkle—the feathery
whisper of her father's encouragement,

ochre—the warmth
of her father's hand
as they strolled in the country,

cobalt and crystal—
the summers splashing
in the ocean's waves.

Helen began to paint again.
And eventually, art healed her.

Helen followed the rules well enough to succeed in school and go to college to study painting.

Her professor wanted colors separated with thick black lines, her brush marks and planes arranged across her canvas to create depth and space.

Helen loved college but longed to paint what she *felt* inside. Painting feelings couldn't be contained in black lines or organized into clear shapes or objects.

Helen dreamed of setting her colors free, like she
was as a child, running without boundaries.

She searched for more.

After college, Helen moved back to New York where many artists were exploring forms, lines, and shapes differently. They overlapped bands of color, thought more about geometry, and painted larger and larger pictures.

Helen met an artist named Jackson Pollock, whose paintings hung in museums and galleries. The art world called him *the greatest living painter in the United States*.

Reviewers celebrated him. Fans loved him. When Helen saw his work, she marveled at how he splattered and dripped his paints on canvas tacked to the studio floor.

If he broke the rules, why couldn't she?

Helen exhibited her art in small shows while male painters were given larger exhibits. Critics called Helen's work *too sweet in color, too lyrical, too ladylike.*

She worked longer and harder at her paintings, drawing strength from her memories of the country and sea. She wanted to leap into her colors, feel the colors, and be the colors.

Art never let her down.

Helen traveled to Nova Scotia to get away. As she walked through the fields, colors swirled around her. Cerulean blue and coral cascaded down mountains of saffron and gold. Rose, pink, and lavender rippled across the sky. Spring green and vermillion gushed through the sea waves.

Helen felt the countryside move within her body.

She saw the mountains with her arms.

She heard the sea in her wrists.

Could she paint the beauty she saw all around her?

Could color *be* the painting?

Helen grew brave.

Back home in New York, Helen laid a HUGE canvas on the floor.

She put down her brush.

Helen blended red and yellow to make orange,

blues and yellows became greens.

She mixed, and mixed, and mixed

rainbows!

Helen swirled charcoal lines across her canvas to guide her,

like the chalk lines she drew as a girl in the city.

With a fistful of pink, Helen turned her wrist outward and spread the paint—

streams of color racing and

S-P-I-R-A-L-I-N-G.

The paint
S-O-A-K-I-N-G into the canvas,

like rain S-E-E-P-I-N-G into soil.

Helen grabbed a bucket of crimson and . . .

POU

. . . setting her colors FREE.

They RAN
and RUSHED.

The colors turned into memories.

Helen imagined the mountain peaks of Nova Scotia with her arms.

She remembered the sea's waves with her wrists.

With a SWEEP of her arm, she splashed green like sea-foam.

Colors jetéd across the painting,
merged and connected,
like rivers into oceans,
colors into feelings.
Wherever the paint landed was the
perfect place to be.

Grabbing a nearby mop as her partner, Helen promenaded through puddles and pools of paints, pushing and pulling her colors together.

Oranges and reds tangoed,

corals pirouetted,

pinks pliéd,

yellows
and blues
sashayed.

Winding

turning

Spinning

When she was done, Helen danced in that field, free among all the shimmering colors of her life, extending, reaching beyond the painting into forever.

More About Helen Frankenthaler

(Abstract Expressionism, Color Field Painting)

As a child, Helen Frankenthaler lived in New York City with her parents and two sisters. Frankenthaler's father, a judge on the New York State Supreme Court, and her mother realized early on that Frankenthaler was special and fostered their daughter's artistic talents. During summer vacations, Frankenthaler spent time in the countryside with her family where she fell in love with nature—the mountains, sky, and sea. She cherished these memories throughout her life, and they are often reflected in her work.

When Frankenthaler's father died when she was eleven, she fell into despair and suffered with migraines. She struggled in her studies at two private schools, the Horace Mann School and the Brearley School, until she attended the Dalton School for one year and graduated early at age sixteen. At the Dalton School, Frankenthaler studied art with Rufino Tamayo who was an important teacher for her, introducing her to modernism. He was sympathetic and supportive, encouraging her in ways other teachers hadn't before. Tamayo helped Frankenthaler find her way, setting her on the path toward the artist she would become. She then went on to earn a BA from Bennington College, studying under Paul Feeley. According to John Elderfield in his book, *Frankenthaler*, Frankenthaler was inspired by Cubism at Bennington, learning how "brush marks and planes, organized across flat surfaces, create dimension and tonal spaces which appear to move forward and retreat backward in order to represent depth" (Elderfield, 15). Additionally, in 1949, Frankenthaler produced black-and-white pencil drawings under Wallace Harrison. These "intensely worked-over drawings on notepaper were erased, worked-over some more, arranged and then rearranged" (Elderfield, 17), fully demonstrating Frankenthaler's understanding of tone and color with only a pencil!

After college, Helen Frankenthaler met Jackson Pollock. It was then she began experimenting with technique. She developed the "soak-stain" method where she thinned her oil paints and poured them onto an unprimed canvas, allowing them to soak through the canvas. Frankenthaler followed her

Mountains and Sea, 1952. Oil and charcoal on unsized, unprimed canvas. 86⅜ x 117¼ inches (219.4 X 297.8 cm). Helen Frankenthaler Foundation, N.Y. On extended loan to the National Gallery of Art, Washington, D.C. © 2019 Helen Frankenthaler Foundation, Inc. / Artists Rights Society (ARS), New York.

inspiration and used this technique with her game-changing 7'x10' painting, *Mountains and Sea* (1952), which she painted all in one day's work after a vacation in Nova Scotia. She dated the painting 10/26/52. Although it is unknown if she had a plan for *Mountains and Sea*, her swirling charcoal lines suggest she did plan some of it beforehand. Frankenthaler poured her oil paints thinned with turpentine onto a very large unprimed canvas, allowing them to run free and to soak into the fibers, creating luminous, radiant "fields of color." The paints became the canvas. The canvas became the painting.

Often, in her work over the decades, Helen Frankenthaler controlled the flow of paint with a variety of tools like sponges, sponge-mops on long handles, large brushes, and squeegees. Helen Frankenthaler was a supreme colorist. Because of her technique and the huge size of her paintings, Frankenthaler moved around the canvas as she worked, reaching in with her wrists and arms like a dancer performing on stage. Frankenthaler's "soak-stain" paintings changed the course of abstract art, ushering in an entirely new movement in art: Color Field painting. Frankenthaler's work can be seen in almost every major museum of modern art in the United States and elsewhere in the world.

Besides her "soak-stain" technique, Helen Frankenthaler worked in prints (especially woodcuts), sculpture, and ceramics. Her work remained tied to nature and human emotions. Helen Frankenthaler became one of the major Abstract Expressionists of the twentieth century, according to leading art historians.

Timeline

December 12, 1928: Helen Frankenthaler is born in New York, New York.

1945: Graduates from the Dalton School in New York, New York.

1946–1949: Studies art at Bennington College, Bennington, Vermont, earns a BA.

1950: Meets art critic Clement Greenberg who introduces her to leading figures in the New York art world, including Jackson Pollock.

October 26, 1952: Paints *Mountains and Sea*.

1953: Greenberg takes painters Morris Louis and Kenneth Noland to Frankenthaler's studio where they see *Mountains and Sea*. They are influenced by the visit and begin painting in the style to become known as the Color Field Movement.

1958: Marries artist Robert Motherwell (divorced in 1971).

1960s–1990s: Frankenthaler teaches and gives seminars at Harvard, University of Pennsylvania, Columbia University, Princeton, Yale, Cornell, Bennington College, Hunter College, and many more.

1960: First retrospective of paintings at the Jewish Museum, New York, New York.

1969: Retrospective of paintings at the Whitney Museum of American Art, New York, New York, which travels to England and Germany.

1980: Retrospective of prints at the Sterling and Francine Clark Art Institute, Williamstown, Massachusetts, which travels throughout the United States.

1985: Retrospective of works on paper at the Solomon R. Guggenheim Museum in New York, New York, which travels throughout the United States.

1989: Retrospective of paintings at the Museum of Modern Art in New York, New York, organized by the Modern Art Museum of Fort Worth, and travels throughout the United States.

1993: Retrospective of prints at the National Gallery of Art, Washington, D.C., which travels throughout the United States.

2001: Awarded the National Medal of Arts.

2002: Retrospective of woodcuts at the Naples Art Museum, Florida, which travels throughout the United States and Japan.

2003: Retrospective of works on paper at the Museum of Contemporary Art, Miami, Florida, which travels to Edinburgh, Scotland.

December 27, 2011: Frankenthaler dies at her home in Darien, Connecticut.

Poured Paint/Soak-Stain Activity

Materials:
- White paper
- Watercolor paints
- Small paint containers or buckets
- Different sized paintbrushes
- Different sized sponges, some can be on the ends of sticks
- Mop, squeegee, and a turkey baster
- Pencil (for possible sketching of an idea)
- Plastic garbage bag or other protective covering

Creating Your Painting:
- Prepare your work area. Cover it with a garbage bag.
- Select your colors of paint and mix the paint with water in the containers (approximately 1 tablespoon of paint mixed with water—thin the paint to your preference; mix colors together to create new ones!).
- Hold a sheet of paper underwater to get it wet, and then let the excess water drip off.
- Place the paper flat on your work space.
- Think about your painting. What do you want to paint? What do you wish to express? What do you want your colors to be? What feeling, memory, or emotion do you want to capture?
- Begin by pouring your colors and letting them blend, soak, and "dance" together on the paper.
- Pour water onto the canvas.
  Note: Don't be afraid to use LOTS of water. Notice how the amount of water changes the color or results in new colors.
- Move yourself around the painting and look at it from all sides. Let your arms sway, dance, sweep, and jolt. How do these movements change how the paint is applied to the canvas? Like Helen, *reach in* with your arms and wrists.
- Use mops, squeegees, a turkey baster, and sponges to guide and control the flow of paint.
- For larger projects or group/class art activities, use larger sheets of paper or a large unprimed canvas like Helen Frankenthaler.
- Your painting can be whatever you want it to be. Be daring. Be curious. Have fun. Invent your own way to paint. Try new things. Remember, there are no rules!

Author's Note

I will never forget standing in front of *Mountains and Sea* in the National Gallery of Art in Washington, D.C. Helen Frankenthaler's paints swirl and dance on the canvas, as if they are floating in air. I first learned about Frankenthaler and her art in college. I was lucky enough to have an art history professor in a contemporary art history course who loved Frankenthaler's work, showed the class her paintings, and helped us understand her concepts and techniques in relationship to what else was happening in the post-war modern art world.

Frankenthaler's paintings and ideas continue to shape the visions of young artists everywhere. This is what inspired me to write this book. Helen Frankenthaler's technique is used in K–12 art education programs and in art courses from preschool through professional level. My own daughter created artwork with Frankenthaler's method beginning in preschool and then continued to do "soak-stain" and poured paint activities in both her school art courses as well as her extracurricular art classes. She was excited to work in such a free, fun, and colorful art practice. I was truly able to see how Frankenthaler's painting techniques have inspired artists and art lovers everywhere, even young children. And once again, I felt the same experience of floating on air, just as I do whenever I see a Frankenthaler painting.

Throughout her life, Frankenthaler was inspired by colors, light, movement, shapes, and nature, all of which helped her create *Mountains and Sea* and her other works. What inspires you?

Quotes and Sources

"There are no rules. That is how art is born, how breakthroughs happen. Go against the rules or ignore the rules. That is what invention is all about." "Helen Frankenthaler Foundation – Biography." Helen Frankenthaler Foundation, 2015. www.frankenthalerfoundation.org/.

[Is he] "the greatest living painter in the United States?" "Jackson Pollock." *LIFE*. 8 Aug. 1949: 42.

[According to John Elderfield in his book, *Frankenthaler*, Frankenthaler was inspired by Cubism at Bennington, learning how] "brush marks and planes, organized across flat surfaces, create dimension and tonal spaces which appear to move forward and retreat backward in order to represent depth." Elderfield, John. *Frankenthaler*. New York: Abrams, 1989.

[These] "intensely worked-over drawings on notepaper were erased, worked-over some more, arranged and then rearranged." Elderfield, John. *Frankenthaler*. New York: Abrams, 1989.

Select Bibliography

Primary:

Elderfield, John. *Frankenthaler*. New York: Abrams, 1989.

Frankenthaler, Helen. Interview by Louise Sweeney. *The Christian Science Monitor*, 1980.

Frankenthaler, Helen. "Interview with Helen Frankenthaler." Grolier Multimedia Encyclopedia, 1995. YouTube, January 12, 2012.

Frankenthaler, Helen. *Mountains and Sea*. 1952, oil and charcoal on unsized, unprimed canvas, 86⅜" x 117¼". Helen Frankenthaler Foundation, New York, on extended loan to the National Gallery of Art, Washington, D.C.

Frankenthaler, Helen. "Oral History Interview with Helen Frankenthaler, 1968." Interview by Barbara Rose. Archives of American Art, Smithsonian Institution, 1968. Web.

Painters Painting. Dir. Emile De Antonio. Perf. Helen Frankenthaler, et al. New York Art Scene 1940–1970. New Video, 1973. DVD.

Remarks and Conversations with Helen Frankenthaler (1972). Dir. Ed Du Vivier and Mel Katz. Perf. Helen Frankenthaler. Portland State University, Special Collections, 1974. Web.

Toward a New Climate. Dir. Perry Miller Adato. WNET, 1978. DVD.

Secondary:

Agee, William C. "Masterpiece: Frankenthaler's New Way of Making Art." *The Wall Street Journal*. November 8, 2008. www.wsj.com/articles/SB122609409221009463.

Carmean, E. A. *Helen Frankenthaler: A Paintings Retrospective*. New York: Abrams, 1989.

Duggan, Bob. "How Helen Frankenthaler Blossomed Into a Great Artist." *Big Think*, 2011. www.bigthink.com/Picture-This/how-helen-frankenthaler-blossomed-into-a-great-artist.

Elderfield, John. *Painted on 21st Street: Helen Frankenthaler from 1950 to 1959*. New York: Gagosian Gallery, 2013.

Fine, Ruth. *Helen Frankenthaler: Prints*. Washington: National Gallery of Art, 1993.

Frankenthaler, Helen. *After Mountains and Sea: Frankenthaler 1956–1959*. New York: Guggenheim Museum, 1998.

Gagosian Gallery. "A Conversation on Helen Frankenthaler: Posing with Color, Paintings 1962–1963." YouTube, September 5, 2014.

Gluck, Grace. "Helen Frankenthaler, Abstract Painter Who Shaped a Movement, Dies at 83." *The New York Times*, December 27, 2011.

Goldman, Judith. *Frankenthaler: The Woodcuts*. Florida: Naples Museum of Art, 2002.

Harrison, Pegram, and Suzanne Boorsch. *Frankenthaler: Prints 1961–1994. A Catalogue Raisonné*. New York: Abrams, 1996.

"Helen Frankenthaler (American, 1928–2011)." *Helen Frankenthaler on Artnet*. Artnet Worldwide Corporation, 2015. www.artnet.com/artists/helen-frankenthaler/.

"Helen Frankenthaler Biography, Art, and Analysis of Works." *The Art Story*. The Art Story Foundation, 2014. www.theartstory.org/artist-frankenthaler-helen.htm.

"Helen Frankenthaler: Biography." Baker Sponder Gallery, accessed July 24, 2015. www.bakerspondergallery.com/artist/Helen_Frankenthaler/biography/.

Marlow, Tim. "Making Painting: Helen Frankenthaler and JMW Turner. Art Experts Discuss Helen Frankenthaler's Artwork" (Audio blog post). Helen Frankenthaler Foundation, January 25, 2014.

Munro, Eleanor C. *Originals: American Women Artists*. New York: Simon and Schuster, 1979.

Robert Motherwell and the New York School: Storming the Citadel. Dir. Catherine Tatge. Perf. Clement Greenberg, William Rubin, and Robert Motherwell. Kultur Video, 2010. DVD.

Rose, Barbara. *Frankenthaler*. New York: Abrams, 1972.

Rowley, Alison. *Helen Frankenthaler: Painting History, Writing Painting*. London: I. B. Tauris, 2007.

Wilkin, Karen. *Frankenthaler Works on Paper: A Retrospective, 1949–84*. New York: G. Braziller, 1984.

Other:

Helen Frankenthaler Foundation. Helen Frankenthaler Foundation (website), 2015. www.frankenthalerfoundation.org/.

Madani, Jennifer. "Helen Frankenthaler for Kids." Pinterest (website), accessed June 20, 2015. www.pinterest.com/jnmadani/helen-frankenthaler-for-kids/.

For my daughter
—E.B.

For Jane, Mandy, and Cecilia
—A.S.

"There are no rules. That is how art is born, how breakthroughs happen. Go against the rules or ignore the rules. That is what invention is all about."

—HELEN FRANKENTHALER

The artwork for this book was created with watercolor, ink, and charcoal pencil.

Library of Congress Cataloging-in-Publication Data

Names: Brown, Elizabeth, 1964- | Sicuro, Aimée, 1976- illustrator.
Title: Dancing through fields of color: the story of Helen Frankenthaler / by Elizabeth Brown; illustrated by Aimée Sicuro.
Description: New York : Abrams Books for Young Readers, 2019.
Identifiers: LCCN 2018015130 | ISBN 978-1-4197-3-4106 (hardcover with jacket)
Subjects: LCSH: Frankenthaler, Helen, 1928-2011—Juvenile literature. | Painters—United States—Biography—Juvenile literature. | Women painters—United States—Biography—Juvenile literature.
Classification: LCC ND237.F675 B76 2019 | DDC 759.13 [B]—dc23

Text copyright © 2019 Elizabeth Brown
Illustrations copyright © 2019 Aimée Sicuro
Book design by Pamela Notarantonio

Printed and bound in China
10 9 8 7 6 5 4 3 2 1

Abrams Books for Young Readers are available at special discounts when purchased in quantity for premiums and promotions as well as fundraising or educational use. Special editions can also be created to specification. For details, contact specialsales@abramsbooks.com or the address below.

Abrams® is a registered trademark of Harry N. Abrams, Inc.

ABRAMS The Art of Books
195 Broadway, New York, NY 10007
abramsbooks.com